Key Words German

Ian MacDonald

Contents

Longman

D0755316

Town Life

Common Landmarks in Town

die Brücke (-n)	bridge
der Bürgersteig (-e)	pavement
der Busbahnhof (=e)	bus station
der Dom (-e)	cathedral
die Einbahnstraße (-n)	one-way street
die Haltestelle (-n)	bus/tram stop
die Hauptstraße (-n)	main street
das Hotel (-s)	hotel
das Kaufhaus (=er)	department store
das Kino (-s)	cinema
die Kirche (-n)	church
das Krankenhaus (=er)	hospital
die Kreuzung (-en)	crossroads
der Markt (=e)	market
das Museum (Museen)	museum
der Park (-s)	park
das Parkhaus (=er)	multi-storey car park
das Postamt (=er)	post office
das Rathaus (=er)	town hall
das Restaurant (-s)	restaurant
die Stadtmitte (-n)	town centre
die Tankstelle (-n)	filling station
das Theater (-)	theatre
die U-Bahn (-en)	underground railway
der Verkehr	traffic
das Verkehrsamt (=er)	tourist information office
der Wohnblock (-s)	block of flats
der Zeitungskiosk (-e)	newspaper stand

Shops

die Apotheke (-n)	dispensing chemist's
die Bäckerei (-en)	bakery
das Blumengeschäft (-e)	flower shop
die Buchhandlung (-en)	bookshop
die Drogerie (-n)	chemist's
die Eisenwarenhandlung (-en)	ironmonger's
die Fischhandlung (-en)	fishmonger's
die Fleischerei (-en)	butcher's
der Gemüsehändler (-)	greengrocer's
das Juweliergeschäft (-e)	jeweller's
die Konditorei (-en)	cake shop
der Laden (∸)	shop
das Lebensmittelgeschäft (-e)	grocery
das Reformhaus (∸er)	health food shop
die Reinigung (-en)	cleaner's
das Reisebüro (-s)	travel agent's
das Schreibwarengeschäft (-e)	stationer's
das Schuhgeschäft (-e)	shoe shop
der Souvenirladen (∸)	souvenir shop
das Sportgeschäft (-e)	sports shop
der Supermarkt (∸e)	supermarket
der Süßwarenladen (∸)	sweet shop
der Tabakladen (∸)	tobacconist's
die Tierhandlung (-en)	pet shop
das Warenhaus (∸er)	department store
die Weinhandlung (-en)	off-licence
der Zeitungshändler (-)	newsagent

At the Post Office

der Brief (-e)	letter
der Briefkasten (-)	letter box
die Briefmarke (-n)	stamp
der Briefträger (-)/	postman/woman
die Briefträgerin (-nen)	
der Einschreibebrief (-e)	registered letter
das Ferngespräch (-e)	trunk call
der Fernsprecher (-)	telephone
die Fernsprechzelle (-n)	telephone kiosk
das Formular (-e)	form
der Luftpostbrief (-e)	air mail letter
das Paket (-e)	parcel
die Paketpost	parcel post
die Post (-en)	post, post office
das Postamt (-er)	post office
die Postanweisung (-en)	postal order
das Postauto (-s)	post van
der Postbeamte (-n)/	post-office clerk
die Postbeamtin (-nen)	
die Postkarte (-n)	postcard
der Postsack (-e)	mailbag
das Ortsgespräch (-e)	local telephone call
der Schalter (-)	counter
das Telegramm (-e)	telegram
der Umschlag (-e)	envelope

die Leitung ist besetzt	the line is engaged
die Nummer wählen	to dial the number
ein Formular ausfüllen	to fill out a form
ein Telegramm schicken	to send a telegram
ich bin falsch verbunden	I've got the wrong number
jemanden anrufen	to telephone someone
wer ist am Apparat?	who's calling?

3

At a Hotel

das Badezimmer (-)	bathroom
der Balkon (-s)	balcony
die Bar (-s)	bar
die Bedienung	service
das Doppelzimmer (-)	double room
die Dusche (-n)	shower
das Einzelzimmer (-)	single room
der Empfangschef (-s)/	reception clerk/receptionist
die Empfangsdame (-n)	
die Empfangshalle (-n)	foyer
der Gast (–e)	guest
das Gepäck	luggage
das Hotel (-s)	hotel
der Kellner (-)	waiter
der Lift (-s)	lift
die Rechnung (-en)	bill
das Restaurant (-s)	restaurant
das Schwimmbad (–er)	swimming pool
das Speisezimmer (-)	dining room
der Stockwerk (-e)	floor, storey
der Träger (-)	porter
das Zimmermädchen (-)	chambermaid

bestellen	to book
das Anmeldeformular ausfüllen	to fill in the register
Halbpension	half board
ich habe unter dem Namen	I have reserved a room
Schmidt reservieren lassen	in the name of Smith
im zweiten Stock	on the second floor
mit Blick aufs Meer	with a sea view
sich anmelden	to register
Vollpension	full board
wie lange bleiben Sie?	how long are you staying?

4

Cinema and Theatre

der Balkon (-s)	balcony
die Bühne (-n)	stage
der Film (-e)	film
der Filmstar (-s)	film star
die Handlung (-en)	action, plot
die Karte (-n)	ticket
die Kasse (-n)	box office
die Komödie (-n)	comedy
der Krimi (-s)	detective film
das Parkett	stalls
die Pause (-n)	interval
der Platzanweiser (-)/	usher/usherette
die Platzanweiserin (-nen)	
der Regisseur (-e)	producer
der Schauspieler (-)/	actor/actress
die Schauspielerin (-nen)	
das Stück (-e)	play
die Tragödie (-n)	tragedy
die Vorstellung (-en)	performance
der Western (-s)	western
die Zuschauer (pl.)	audience

aufregend	exciting
ausverkauft	sold out
eine Rolle spielen	to play a part
im ersten Rang	in the first row
in der Hauptrolle	in the leading role
klatschen	to clap
komisch	funny
langweilig	boring
unterhaltend	entertaining
vorbestellen	to reserve
was läuft?	what's on?

Exercise 1
What happens where?

Match each phrase from the left-hand column with a phrase chosen from the right-hand column to make the best sense.

1. An einer Tankstelle
2. Im Kino
3. An der Kasse
4. An einer Haltestelle
5. In einem Blumengeschäft
6. Der Briefträger
7. In einem Reisebüro
8. In einem Süßwarenladen
9. In einem Restaurant
10. In einem Postamt

a. wartet man auf eine Straßenbahn oder einen Bus.
b. kann man Benzin tanken.
c. läuft ein amerikanischer Film.
d. kauft man Rosen und Tulpen.
e. kann man Briefmarken kaufen.
f. bringt der Kellner die Speisekarte.
g. verkauft man Bonbons.
h. kann man seine Ferien buchen.
i. bringt uns Briefe und Pakete.
j. sagt man, daß die Vorstellung schon ausverkauft ist.

Exercise 2
Odd Man Out

Choose the odd man out in each of the following groups of words. Give your reasons for selecting it.

1. Bäckerei   Fischhandlung   Parkhaus   Weinhandlung
2. Telegramm   Brief   Tabakladen   Paket
3. Balkon   Rechnung   Badezimmer   Dusche
4. Empfangsdame   Schauspieler   Zuschauer   Platzanweiserin
5. Speisesaal   Restaurant   Konditorei   Schwimmbad

Exercise 3
Missing Letters

Fill in the blank spaces with German words to suit the clues.
Another German word will emerge inside the oval. What is it?

1. Send one if you have an
   urgent message
2. Put one on your
   envelope
3. Take a cold one
4. A large store
5. Buy bottles of drink here

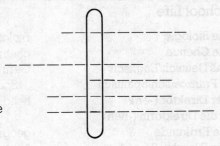

Exercise 4
True or False?

Decide whether you think the following statements are true or false.

1. In einem Hotel gibt es Einzelzimmer und Doppelzimmer.
2. In einem Verkehrsamt kann man gut essen und trinken.
3. Bei einem Gemüsehändler kauft man Blumenkohl und Karotten.
4. Wenn man jemanden anrufen will, muß man zuerst die Nummer
   wählen.
5. Der Kellner bringt Ihnen die Rechnung, bevor Sie ein Zimmer
   buchen.

Exercise 5
Jumbled Words

Use the clues to unravel these jumbled German words.

1. Makes you laugh in the theatre.   I M O K Ö D E
2. The action takes place here.   N E B Ü H
3. Do this to show appreciation.   H C K S L T A E N
4. Do this to ensure a seat.   N E L V R B O E S T E L
5. A letter will come through here.   E A K F R B I E S T N
6. Not a long distance call.   P G R E Ä S C H O T S R
7. Buy your paper here.   K S G Z I N U I O E S T K
8. Fill up here!   L A E T K N S T L E
9. Might cross a river.   E K B Ü R C
10. Holiday mementoes here.   N L V O E S N U A R I D E

Topic 2
The World of Work

School Life

die Biologie	biology
die Chemie	chemistry
das Deutsch/Englisch/ Französisch/Spanisch	German/English/French/ Spanish
der Direktor (-en)/ die Direktorin (-nen)	headmaster/headmistress
die Erdkunde	geography
der Filzschreiber (-)	felt-tip pen
die Geschichte	history
die Grundschule (-n)	primary school
das Gymnasium (Gymnasien)	grammar school
die Hausaufgabe (-n)	homework
der Hof (¨e)	playground
die Kantine (-n)	canteen
die Klasse (-n)	class
das Klassenzimmer (-)	classroom
der Kuli (-s)	ball-point pen
die Kunst	art
der Lehrer (-)/ die Lehrerin (-nen)	teacher
das Lieblingsfach (¨er)	favourite subject
die Mathe	maths
die Musik	music
die Pause (-n)	break
die Prüfung (-en)	examination
der Schreibtisch (-e)	desk
der Schüler (-)/ die Schülerin (-nen)	schoolboy/girl
das Schulzeugnis (-se)	report
das (Sprach)labor (-s)	(language) laboratory
die Stunde (-n)	lesson
der Test (-s)	test

---

eine gute/schlechte Note	a good/bad mark

8

Out at Work

der Architekt (-en)/ die Architektin (-nen)	architect
der Bergarbeiter (-)	miner
der/die Büroangestellte (-n)	office worker
der Elektriker (-)	electrician
der Empfangschef (-s)/ die Empfangsdame (-n)	reception clerk/receptionist
der Fensterputzer (-)	window cleaner
der Feuerwehrmann (¨er)	fireman
der Fotograf (-en)	photographer
der Friseur (-e)	barber
die Friseuse (-n)	hairdresser
der Geschäftsmann (¨er)/ die Geschäftsfrau (-en)	businessman/woman
die Geschäftsleute	business people
der Ingenieur (-e)	engineer
der Journalist (-en)/ die Journalistin (-nen)	journalist
der Klempner (-)	plumber
der Koch (¨e)/die Köchin (-nen)	cook
der Lehrer (-)/die Lehrerin (-nen)	teacher
der LKW-Fahrer (-)	lorry driver
der Mechaniker (-)	mechanic
der Polizist (-en)/die Polizistin (-nen)	policeman/woman
die Putzfrau (-en)	cleaning lady
der Rechtsanwalt (¨e)/ die Rechtsanwältin (-nen)	lawyer
der Reporter (-)/ die Reporterin (-nen)	reporter
der Richter (-) die Richterin (-nen)	judge
die Sekretärin (-nen)	secretary
die Stenotypistin (-nen)	shorthand typist
der Taxifahrer (-)	taxi driver
der Tierarzt (¨e)/die Tierärztin (-nen)	vet
der Tischler (-)	carpenter
der Verkäufer (-)/ die Verkäuferin (-nen)	sales assistant
der Vertreter (-)	rep

Exercise 1
Missing Words

Choose a suitable word from the School Life word-list to complete the following sentences.

1. Im Klassenzimmer sitzt der Lehrer hinter einem _____.
2. Mein Lieblingsfach ist _____.
3. Mein Kuli ist kaputt. Ich muß mit einem _____ schreiben.
4. Meine kleine Schwester ist erst sechs Jahre alt. Sie geht zur _____.
5. Nach dieser Stunde haben wir zehn Minuten _____.
6. Es sind dreißig _____ in meiner Klasse.
7. Zu Mittag essen wir alle in der _____.
8. Dann stehen wir mit unseren Freunden auf dem _____ und sprechen miteinander.
9. Der Lehrer gibt uns eine _____ für heute nachmittag.
10. Die nächste Stunde ist Englisch. Unsere Klasse geht dann ins _____.

Exercise 2
Occupations

Study the clues and decide which occupation is being described.

1. Er macht Fotos. → FOTOGRAF
2. Sie arbeitet in einem Büro, sitzt vor einer Schreibmaschine und tippt. → ?
3. Er schreibt Artikel für eine Zeitung. → ?
4. Man findet diese Dame in einem Hotel. Hoffentlich sagt sie: „Ja, ich habe ein Zimmer frei!" → ?
5. Er arbeitet im Bergwerk und schürft Kohle. → ?
6. Sie gehen zu ihm, wenn Ihr Hund oder Ihre Katze krank ist. → ?
7. Vielleicht macht er Tische, Stühle usw. → ?
8. Er/sie arbeitet in einem Klassenzimmer. → ?
9. Sie suchen ihn, wenn Sie sehr schnell zum Bahnhof fahren müssen. → ?
10. Er/sie arbeitet in einem Restaurant und bereitet das Essen zu. → ?

Topic 3
Seaside and Countryside

At the Seaside

der Bikini (-s)	bikini
das Boot (-e)	boat
die Bucht (-en)	bay
der Jachthafen (˸)	marina
die Klippe (-n)	cliff
die Küste (-n)	coast
die Luftmatratze (-n)	airbed
das Meer (-e)	sea
die Möwe (-n)	seagull
der Sand (-e)	sand
die Sandburg (-en)	sandcastle
das Schiff (-e)	ship
die See (-n)	sea
die Sonne (-n)	sun
der Sonnenschirm (-e)	parasol
der Strand (˸e)	beach
der Strandkorb (˸e)	wicker beach chair
das Wasser	water
die Welle (-n)	wave
das Windsurfen	windsurfing

an die See fahren	to go to the seaside
angeln	to fish
baden	to bathe
liegen	to lie
mieten	to hire
schwimmen	to swim
segeln	to sail
tauchen	to dive
ruhig	calm
auf offenem Meer	on the high sea, out at sea

11

In the Countryside

der Bach (÷e)	brook
der Bauernhof (÷e)	farmyard
der Baum (÷e)	tree
die Brücke (-n)	bridge
das Dorf (÷er)	village
der Fluß (Flüsse)	river
der Gasthof (÷e)	inn
der Gipfel (-)	hilltop
der Graben (÷)	ditch
die Jugendherberge (-n)	youth hostel
die Hecke (-n)	hedge
die Heide (-n)	heath, moor
der Hügel (-)	hill
die Landschaft (-en)	countryside, landscape
die Landstraße (-n)	highway
der Pfad (-e)	path
der See (-n)	lake
der Stein (-e)	stone
der Sumpf (÷e)	marsh
das Tal (÷er)	valley
der Teich (-e)	pond
das Tor (-e)	gate
das Ufer (-)	bank
der Wald (÷er)	wood
der Wasserfall (÷e)	waterfall
der Weg (-e)	path
der Wegweiser (-)	signpost
die Wiese (n)	meadow

auf dem Lande sein	to be in the countryside
aufs Land fahren	to go into the country
bergauf/bergab gehen	to go uphill/downhill

12

Exercise 1
Likely or Not?

Decide whether the following statements are likely or not! (The exercise is based on seaside vocabulary.)

Gestern fuhr ich mit meinem Bruder und einigen Freunden an die See. Es war ein herrlicher Tag und . . . .

1. Wir nahmen sofort ein Sonnenbad.
2. Mein Bruder Max zog seinen Bikini an.
3. Wir konnten in der Bucht ein Motorboot mieten.
4. Viele Möwen flogen im Jachthafen umher.
5. Die See war sehr ruhig. Die Wellen waren also ziemlich hoch.
6. Auf dem Sand konnten wir drei Stunden lang schwimmen.
7. Im Hafen konnte ich angeln gehen.
8. Viele Fischerboote waren auf offenem Meer zu sehen.
9. Im Wasser bauten wir eine schöne Sandburg.

Exercise 2
Missing Verbs

Put all the verbs below into the sentences where they will make sense. (The exercise is based on seaside vocabulary.)

angeln baden bauen sitzen fliegen mieten schwimmen
surfen tauchen

1. Sehen Sie, wie die Vögel ins Wasser _____, um Fische zu fangen?
2. Drei junge Mädchen _____ in der See.
3. Für mich ist das Wasser viel zu kalt. Ich gehe nicht _____.
4. Mein Vater und meine Mutter _____ in einem Strandkorb und lesen Zeitungen.
5. Im Jachthafen kann man kleine Boote _____.
6. Möchten Sie einen Hafenrundflug machen, oder werden Sie luftkrank, wenn Sie _____?
7. Hier gibt es nicht genug Sand, um eine Sandburg zu _____.
8. Zu Weihnachten wünsche ich mir ein Surfbrett. Dann gehe ich jeden Tag _____.
9. Sehen Sie die Jungen, die da drüben _____? Sie haben schon fünf Fische gefangen!

13

Exercise 3
Missing Letters

Use the clues to help you fill in the blanks, and an extra word will finally emerge in the oval shape. Give its meaning in English. (This exercise is based on countryside vocabulary.)

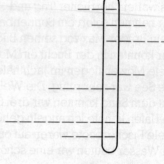

1. Ein anderes Wort für Pfad
2. Wächst in einem Wald
3. Achtung! Alles ist hier so naß!
4. Zwischen zwei Bergen findet man ein . . . .
5. Kleiner See
6. Hier kann man viele Tiere sehen
7. Kleiner als eine Stadt

Exercise 4
Crossword Puzzle

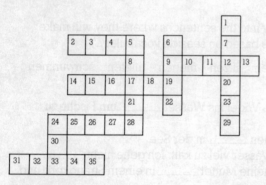

clues across

2. Kleiner als ein Fluß (und Komponist!)
9. Hier kann man angeln gehen
14. Ich fahre über die _____; das ist schneller
24. Voller Gras?
31. Kleiner Berg

clues down

1. Man kann es trinken
5. Eine _____ ist oft grün und wächst zwischen zwei Feldern
6. Der Rhein hat zwei _____
24. Pfad

14

The World of Nature

Birds

der Adler (-)	eagle
die Amsel (-n)	blackbird
die Ente (-n)	duck
die Eule (-n)	owl
die Feder (-n)	feather
der Flügel (-)	wing
die Gans (¨e)	goose
die Henne (-n)	hen
das Huhn (¨er)	chicken
der Kanarienvogel (¨)	canary
die Krähe (n)	crow
der Kuckuck (-e)	cuckoo
die Lerche (-n)	lark
die Möwe (-n)	seagull
die Nachtigall (-en)	nightingale
das Nest (-er)	nest
der Papagei (-en)	parrot
das Rotkehlchen (-)	robin
der Schnabel (¨)	beak
die Schwalbe (-n)	swallow
der Schwan (¨e)	swan
der Spatz (-en)	sparrow
der Star (-e)	starling
der Strauß (-e)	ostrich
die Taube (-n)	dove
der Truthahn (¨e)	turkey
der Vogel (¨)	bird
der Wellensittich (-e)	budgerigar

ein Ei legen	to lay an egg
zwitschern	to twitter

Flowers and Garden

die Blume (-n)	flower
das Blumenbeet (-e)	flower bed
die Erde	earth
der Garten (⸚)	garden
der Gemüsegarten (⸚)	vegetable garden
das Gewächshaus (⸚er)	greenhouse
die Gießkanne (-n)	watering can
das Gras	grass
die Hacke (-n)	hoe
die Hecke (-n)	hedge
die Hütte (-n)	shed
das Maiglöckchen (-)	lily of the valley
die Narzisse (-n)	daffodil
die Nelke (-n)	carnation
der Pfad (-e)	path
die Pflanze (-n)	plant
der Rasen (-)	lawn
der Rasenmäher (-)	lawn mower
die Rose (-n)	rose
das Samenkorn (⸚er)	seed
der Schlauch (⸚e)	hose
der Schubkarren (-)	wheelbarrow
der Stein (-e)	stone
der Strauch (⸚e *or* ⸚er)	shrub
die Tulpe (-n)	tulip
das Unkraut *(sing.)*	weeds
das Vergißmeinnicht	forget-me-not
der Zaun (⸚e)	fence

---

jäten	to weed
umgraben	to dig over

16

Trees

der Ast (¨e)	branch
der Baum (¨e)	tree
die Beere (-n)	berry
die Birke (-n)	birch
das Blatt (¨er)	leaf
die Buche (-n)	beech
der Busch (¨e)	bush
die Eiche (-n)	oak
die Esche (-n)	ash
das Gebüsch (*sing.*)	bushes
das Holz	wood
die Kastanie (-n)	chestnut
die Kiefer (-n)	pine
die Knospe (-n)	bud
das Laubwerk	foliage
der Lindenbaum (¨e)	lime tree
der Obstbaum (¨e)	fruit tree
die Pappel (-n)	poplar
die Platane (-n)	plane tree
die Rinde (-n)	bark
der Stamm (¨e)	trunk
der Tannenbaum (¨e)	fir tree
die Ulme (-n)	elm
der Wald (¨er)	wood, forest
der Weidenbaum (¨e)	willow
der Weihnachtsbaum (¨e)	Christmas tree
der Weinberg (-e)	vineyard
der Wipfel	treetop
die Wurzel (-n)	root
der Zweig (-e)	branch

Insects and Animals

die Ameise (-n)	ant
der Bär (-en)	bear
die Biene (-n)	bee
der Elefant (-en)	elephant
die Fliege (-n)	fly
der Hamster (-)	hamster
der Hirsch (-e)	deer
der Hund (-e)	dog
das Insekt (-en)	insect
der Käfer (-)	beetle
das Kamel (-e)	camel
das Kaninchen (-)	rabbit
die Katze (-n)	cat
die Kuh (¨e)	cow
der Löwe (-n)	lion
die Maus (¨e)	mouse
das Meerschweinchen (-)	guinea pig
das Nashorn (¨er)	rhinoceros
das Nilpferd (-e)	hippopotamus
das Pferd (-e)	horse
das Schaf (-e)	sheep
die Schildkröte (-n)	tortoise
die Schlange (-n)	snake
der Schmetterling (-e)	butterfly
das Schwein (-e)	pig
die Spinne (-n)	spider
der Tiger (-)	tiger
die Wespe (-n)	wasp

fressen	to eat
stechen	to sting

On the Farm

der Bauer (-n)	farmer
das Bauernhaus (¨er)	farmhouse
der Bauernhof (¨e)	farmyard
die Ernte (-n)	harvest
das Feld (-er)	field
das Geflügel	poultry
die Gerste	barley
das Getreide *(sing.)*	cereals
der Hafer *(sing.)*	oats
die Herde (-n)	herd, flock
das Heu	hay
der Heuhaufen (-)	haystack
das Hühnerhaus (¨er)	henhouse
das Korn	corn
der Kuhstall (¨e)	cowshed
der Mähdrescher (-)	combine harvester
die Milchkanne (-n)	milk churn
der Pferdestall (¨e)	stable
der Pflug (¨e)	plough
der Roggen	rye
der Schäferhund (-e)	sheepdog
die Scheune (-n)	barn
der Schuppen (-)	shed
der Schweinestall (¨e)	pigsty
der Stier (-e)	bull
das Stroh	straw
das Vieh	cattle
der Weizen	wheat
die Wiese (-n)	meadow

---

füttern	to feed

Weather

die Aufheiterung (-en)	bright period
der Blitz (-e)	lightning
die Brise (-n)	breeze
der Donner	thunder
der Dunst	haze
das Eis	ice
der Frost (¨e)	frost
das Gewitter (-)	thunderstorm
die Hitze	heat
die Hitzewelle (-n)	heat wave
die Kälte	cold
der Nebel (-)	fog
der Platzregen	downpour
der Regen	rain
der Schauer (-)	shower
der Schnee	snow
der Schneeregen	sleet
die Sonne	sun
der Sonnenschein	sunshine
der Sturm	storm (wind and rain)
das Wetter	weather
der Wind (-e)	wind
die Wolke (-n)	cloud

frieren	to freeze
nebelig	foggy
regnen	to rain
scheinen	to shine
schneien	to snow
sonnig	sunny
wie ist das Wetter?	what's the weather like?
windig	windy

Exercise 1
A Bird Search!

Hidden in this puzzle are the German names of ten (and only ten!) birds. Can you find them all? The words may be concealed horizontally, vertically, diagonally, backwards or forwards, and may even overlap. Viel Spaß!

A	K	T	S	N	A	G	S	R	H	B
T	D	G	C	A	R	B	W	L	T	C
E	M	S	H	I	U	Q	H	C	D	X
L	O	F	W	P	G	A	F	B	A	F
E	B	U	A	T	B	R	L	A	E	C
N	O	Q	N	W	Q	S	R	F	W	E
T	J	E	P	O	H	L	Z	C	B	E
E	U	L	E	D	N	E	M	K	Y	A
X	A	E	U	K	I	R	J	L	V	G
P	N	S	V	G	O	C	M	H	T	S
F	M	M	D	U	R	H	E	N	N	E
V	P	A	P	A	G	E	I	L	O	M
O	G	L	T	C	H	T	N	B	P	D
N	U	S	J	Z	F	A	C	E	Y	R

Exercise 2
Round the Garden

```
              I                 P            F
                   U                   Z
         K                   S
              E                     B           A
   M                            O        G
                                         R           D
         T               L          N
```

You may use the letters above as many times as you want. The object of the game is to make up at least twelve German words for things which can be found in the garden. Off you go!

Exercise 3
Jumbled Animals

See how quickly you can unravel these strange jumbled German animals!

1. HUK
2. FCASH
3. LEMAK
4. NECWISH
5. GERIT

6. SUMA
7. AKZET
8. DPEFR
9. SHANRON
10. RETSHAM

Exercise 4
All Kinds of Weather

Choose one of the ten German 'weather words' at the end of this exercise to complete each of the following sentences and make the best sense. Use each word only once.

1. Letzten Winter fuhr mein Vater nicht sehr oft mit dem Auto ins Büro. Es gab zuviel _____ auf der Straße.
2. Auf dem Lande war alles so schön weiß. _____ lag überall.
3. Es ist heute ein bißchen wärmer. Die _____ beginnt endlich zu scheinen.
4. Letzte Woche brauchten wir nicht in die Schule zu gehen. Wir hatten eine _____ und es war viel zu heiß.
5. Ein dichter _____ hing gestern über der Stadtmitte, und man konnte kaum sehen.
6. Bei diesem _____ kann man sehr gut segeln.
7. Der Regen hört gleich auf. Es ist nur ein _____.
8. Es kann bald regnen. Ich sehe eine große schwarze _____ über deinem Haus.
9. Wegen der _____ mußten wir warme Kleider anziehen.
10. Gestern abend hatten wir ein _____. Es donnerte und blitzte.

Nebel   Wind   Sonne   Hitzewelle   Wolke   Eis   Schauer
Schnee   Kälte   Gewitter

Topic 5
Travel

Going on a Journey

das Gepäck	luggage
die Gesellschaftsreise (-n)	package holiday
die Grenze (-n)	border
der Hafen (-)	harbour
der Kai (-s)	quay
die Landung (-en)	landing
der Liegeplatz (-e)	couchette
der Paß (Pässe)	passport
der Passagier (-e)	passenger
die Paßkontrolle	passport control
der Reisescheck (-s)	traveller's cheque
das Reiseziel (-e)	destination
die Seereise (-n)	sea cruise
die Überfahrt (-en)	crossing
die Verbindung (-en)	connection
der Wechselkurs (-e)	rate of exchange
der Zoll	customs
der Zollbeamte (-n)	customs official

(aus)packen	to (un)pack
buchen	to book
erreichen	to reach
ins Ausland fahren	to go abroad
reisen	to travel
starten	to take off
verlassen	to leave
verzollen	to declare

At the Railway Station

die Abfahrt (-en)	departure
das Abteil (-e)	compartment
die Ankunft (-e)	arrival
die Bahn (-en)	railway
der Bahnhof (-e)	station
der Bahnsteig (-e)	platform
die Fahrkarte (-n)	ticket
der Fahrplan (-e)	timetable
die Fahrt (-en)	journey
der Gepäckträger (-)	porter
das Gleis (-e)	platform, track
der Koffer (-)	suitcase
der Kuli (-s)	luggage trolley
der Platz (-e)	seat
die Reise (-n)	journey
der Schaffner (-)	conductor
der Schalter (-)	ticket office
der Speisewagen (-)	restaurant car
das Taxi (-s)	taxi
der Wartesaal (-säle)	waiting room
der Zug (-e)	train

---

steigen	to climb

---

erste (zweite) Klasse	first (second) class
zweimal Frankfurt	two tickets for Frankfurt
frei	free, vacant
einfach	single
hin und zurück	return
besetzt	occupied
auf welchem Gleis?	on which platform?

At the Airport

der Abflug (-e)	departure
die Ankunftshalle (-n)	arrival lounge
die Besatzung (-en)	crew
das Bodenpersonal	ground staff
der Flug (-e)	flight
der Fluggast (-e)	passenger
der Flughafen (-)	airport
die Flughalle (-n)	air terminal
die Fluginformationstafel (-n)	flight information board
der Fluglotse (-n)	air traffic controller
das Flugzeug (-e)	airplane
das Handgepäck	hand luggage
der Jumbo-jet (-s)	jumbo jet
der Kontrollturm (-e)	control tower
die Landebahn (-en)	runway
die Landung (-en)	landing
der Pilot (-en)	pilot
die Rollbahn (-en)	runway
der Sicherheitsgurt (-e)	safety belt
der Start (-e)	take-off
der Steward (-s)	steward
die Stewardeß (die Stewardessen)	stewardess
die Wartehalle (-n)	departure lounge
der zollfreie Laden	duty-free shop

Ausland-Flüge	international flights
einen Flug buchen	to book a flight
erwartet um 14.00 Uhr	expected at 2 p.m.
gelandet	landed
Inland-Flüge	internal flights

25

Vehicles

das Auto (-s)	car
das Boot (-e)	boat
der Bus (-se)	bus
das Düsenflugzeug (-e)	jet plane
die Fähre (-n)	ferry
das (Fahr)rad (¨er)	cycle
der Hubschrauber (-)	helicopter
die Jacht (-en)	yacht
der Jeep (-s)	jeep
der Krankenwagen (-)	ambulance
der Lieferwagen (-)	delivery van
der LKW	lorry
die Lokomotive (-n)	locomotive
das Luftkissenboot (-e)	hovercraft
das Mofa (-s)	moped
das Motorrad (¨er)	motorbike
der Motorroller (-)	scooter
das Raumschiff (-e)	space ship
das Ruderboot (-e)	rowing boat
das Schiff (-e)	ship
das Segelboot (-e)	sailing boat
der Sessellift (-e)	chair lift
die Straßenbahn (-en)	tram
der Streifenwagen (-)	police car
das Taxi (-s)	taxi
der Traktor (-en)	tractor
das U-Boot (-e)	submarine
der Vergnügungsdampfer (-)	pleasure steamer
der Wagen (-)	car
der Wohnwagen (-)	caravan
der Zug (¨e)	train

Exercise 1
Likely or Not?

Are the following sentences likely to be true or not?

1. Wenn man von England nach Frankreich fährt, ist das Luftkissenboot viel schneller als die Fähre.
2. Der Zollbeamte buchte mir ein schönes Zimmer im Hotel.
3. Ich packte all meine Koffer aus, bevor ich ins Taxi stieg.
4. Es ist besser, Reiseschecks zu verkaufen, wenn man ins Ausland fährt.
5. Seereisen mag ich nicht. Ich werde zu oft seekrank.
6. An der Grenze zwischen Frankreich und Belgien gibt es eine Paßkontrolle.
7. Der Pilot saß noch in der Wartehalle, als sein Jumbo-jet startete.
8. Letzten Sommer fuhren wir mit einem U-Boot nach Spanien.

Exercise 2
A Railway Journey

Select a German word from the list below to fill in each of the gaps and make the best sense. Beware of the extra 'decoy' words!

Letzte Woche mußten mein Freund Rolf und ich nach München fahren. Wir beschlossen, die Reise mit der _____ zu machen. Wir fuhren also mit einem _____ zum _____, kauften unsere _____ am Schalter und gingen dann zum Kiosk, wo wir einige Zeitschriften kauften, die wir während der _____ lesen wollten.

Wir hatten Zeit, Erfrischungen zu kaufen, bevor ein _____ unser schweres Gepäck zum _____ Nummer zwei trug. Unser Zug stand schon da. Wir stiegen in einen _____ ein und suchten schnell ein paar _____. Fast alle waren schon _____, aber endlich fanden wir zwei im letzten _____.

Wir legten unsere _____ ins Gepäcknetz und setzten uns hin. Pünktlich um zehn Uhr verließen wir Augsburg. Nach zwei Stunden _____ waren wir aber beide ein bißchen hungrig und durstig. Wir gingen also in den _____. Um drei Uhr nachmittags kam unser _____ endlich in München an. Wir nahmen unsere Koffer und stiegen _____.

Abteil   Wagen   Bahnsteig   Zug   Abfahrt   Plätze   Reise   aus
Schaffner   Gepäckträger   Bahn   Fahrplan   besetzt
Speisewagen   Koffer   Fahrt   Bahnhof   frei   Fahrkarten
einfach   Kuli   Taxi

Exercise 3
It shouldn't be there!

Study carefully the list of forms of transport given below. Decide as quickly as you can which of them you would be *surprised* to find in your nearest town centre! Work through the list again and again until you can do it faultlessly.

ein Raumschiff
ein Auto
ein Segelboot
ein Lieferwagen
ein Taxi
eine Jacht
ein LKW
ein Luftkissenboot

ein Mofa
ein Vergnügungsdampfer
ein Wohnwagen
ein Ruderboot
ein Fahrrad
ein Bus
ein U-Boot

Exercise 4

GESELLSCHAFTSREISE

Using the letters in this word as many times as you wish – but only these letters – find other German words mentioned in previous lists in this book for:

1. An animal
2. A bird
3. Something found in a hotel
4. Something seen out at sea
5. Something in the countryside
6. Something in the garden
7. A kind of tree
8. An insect
9. A type of grain found on a farm
10. A cause of treacherous road conditions in winter

Home and Family

Around the Home

das Badezimmer (-)	bathroom
der Balkon (-s)	balcony
der Boden (÷)	floor
das Dach (÷er)	roof
die Dachstube (-n)	attic
die Decke (-n)	ceiling
die Dusche (-n)	shower
das Eßzimmer (-)	dining room
das Fenster (-)	window
der Flur (-e)	hall
die Garage (-n)	garage
das Haus (÷er)	house
die Haustür (-en)	front door
der Kamin (-e)	fireplace
der Keller (-)	cellar
die Küche (-n)	kitchen
das Schlafzimmer (-)	bedroom
der Teppich (-e)	carpet
die Toilette (-n)	toilet
die Treppe (-n)	stairs
der Vorhang (÷e)	curtain
die Wand (÷e)	wall
die Wohnung (-en)	flat
das Wohnzimmer (-)	living room
die Zentralheizung	central heating

ich gehe die **Treppe** hinauf/ hinunter	I go upstairs/downstairs
ich sehe zum **Fenster** hinaus	I look out of the window
im dritten **Stock**	on the third floor
im **Erdgeschoß**	on the ground floor
oben/unten	upstairs/downstairs

29

Everyday Household Items

das Abwaschtuch (¨er)	dish cloth
die Bettdecke (-n)	blanket
die Bratpfanne (-n)	frying pan
das Bügeleisen (-)	iron
der Eimer (-)	bucket
der Fön (-e)	hair drier
der Hahn (¨e)	tap
das Handtuch (¨er)	hand towel
die Heizdecke (-n)	electric blanket
der Kamm (¨e)	comb
die Kasserolle (-n)	saucepan
der Kassettenrecorder (-)	cassette recorder
der Kessel (-)	kettle
der Krug (¨e)	jug
der Mülleimer (-)	dustbin
der Papierkorb (¨e)	waste paper basket
der Rasierapparat (-e)	shaver
der Schwamm (¨e)	sponge
die Seife	soap
der Spiegel (-)	mirror
das Spülbecken (-)	sink
der Staubsauger (-)	vacuum cleaner
das Tablett (-e)	tray
der Toaster	toaster
das Waschbecken (-)	wash basin
der Wecker (-)	alarm clock
der Wischlappen (-)	duster
die Zahnbürste (-n)	toothbrush
die Zahnpasta	toothpaste

Furniture and Furnishings

die Badewanne (-n)	bath
das Bett (-en)	bed
das Bild (-er)	picture
das Bücherregal (-e)	bookshelf
der Elektroherd (-e)	electric cooker
der (Farb)fernseher (-)	(colour) television
der Fernsprecher (-)	telephone
die Geschirrspülmaschine (-n)	dishwasher
der Kassettenrecorder (-)	cassette recorder
der Kleiderschrank (¨e)	wardrobe
die Kommode (-n)	chest of drawers
der Kühlschrank (¨e)	fridge
die Lampe (-n)	lamp
der Lehnstuhl (¨e)	armchair
der Mixer (-)	mixer
die Möbel (pl.)	furniture
der Nachttisch (-e)	bedside table
die Nähmaschine (-n)	sewing machine
der Plattenspieler (-)	record player
das Radio (-s)	radio
der Schrank (¨e)	cupboard
der Schreibtisch (-e)	desk
das Sofa (-s)	sofa
die Stereoanlage (-n)	stereo unit
die Tiefkühltruhe (-n)	freezer
das Tonbandgerät (-e)	tape recorder
die Uhr (-en)	clock
der Video-Recorder (-)	video recorder
die Waschmaschine (-n)	washing machine

Tools and Implements

das Bohrgerät (-e)	drill
der Engländer (-)	adjustable spanner
der Flaschenöffner (-)	bottle opener
das Gummiband (÷er)	rubber band
der Hammer (÷)	hammer
die Harke (-n)	rake
der Hobel (-)	plane
der Klebstoff	glue
der Korkenzieher (-)	corkscrew
die Leiter (-n)	ladder
die Nadel (-n)	needle
der Nagel (÷)	nail
der Pinsel (-)	paintbrush
der Reißnagel (÷)	drawing pin
die Säge (-n)	saw
die Schere (-n)	scissors
der Schlüssel (-)	key
die Schnur (÷e)	piece of string
die Schraube (-n)	screw
der Schraubenschlüssel (-)	spanner
der Schraubenzieher (-)	screwdriver
der Spaten (-)	spade
der Tesafilm	sticky tape
das Werkzeug (-e)	tool
die Zange (-n)	pliers

flicken	to mend
kleben	to stick
reparieren	to repair
schneiden	to cut
stopfen	to darn
streichen	to paint

Materials

der Backstein	brick
die Baumwolle	cotton
das Beton	concrete
das Blech	tin
das Blei	lead
der Cord	corduroy
das Eisen	iron
das Glas	glass
das Gold	gold
das Holz	wood
der Kristall	crystal
das Kupfer	copper
das Leder	leather
das Leinen	linen
der Marmor	marble
das Messing	brass
das Metall	metal
das Nylon	nylon
das Papier	paper
die Pappe	cardboard
der Pelz	fur
das Plastik	plastic
der Polyester	polyester
das Porzellan	porcelain
der Samt	velvet
die Seide	silk
das Silber	silver
der Stahl	steel
der Stein	stone
die Wolle	wool

Family

das Baby (-s)	baby
der Bruder (-̈)	brother
die Eltern *(pl.)*	parents
der Enkel (-)	grandson
die Enkel *(pl.)*	grandchildren
die Enkelin (-nen)	granddaughter
das Enkelkind (-er)	grandchild
die Erwachsenen *(pl.)*	grown-ups
die Familie (-n)	family
die Frau (-en)	wife
die Geschwister *(pl.)*	brothers and sisters
die Großmutter (-̈)	grandmother
der Großvater (-̈)	grandfather
das Kind (-er)	child
die Kusine (-n)	cousin (female)
der Mann (-̈er)	husband
die Mutter (-̈)	mother
der Neffe (-n)	nephew
die Nichte (-n)	niece
die Oma	grandma
der Opa	grandad
der Onkel (-)	uncle
der Schwager (-̈)/ die Schwägerin (-nen)	brother-in-law/sister-in-law
die Schwester (-n)	sister
der Schwiegersohn (-̈e)	son-in-law
der Sohn (-̈e)	son
die Tante (-n)	aunt
die Tochter (-̈)	daughter
der Vater (-̈)	father
der/die Verwandte (-n)	relative
der Vetter (-n)	cousin (male)
die Zwillinge *(pl.)*	twins

Exercise 1
Missing Letters

Choose words from the first three lists in this topic to complete the blanks below with the help of the clues provided. Another German word will eventually appear in the oval space indicated.

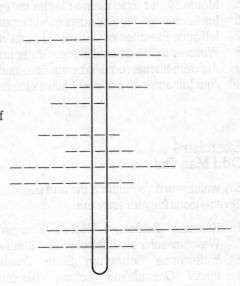

1. You can wash in here
2. You can see through it
3. Found in front of No. 2
4. You can go up it or down it
5. Underground room
6. A home for your car
7. Sit here and enjoy the view
8. On top of a house
9. It'll get you up early if you want it to
10. Wash with it
11. Sleep in here
12. Relax in it
13. Use it for long distance conversation
14. You look into it

Exercise 2
What is it?

Name the German words defined by each of the following clues.

1. Man kämmt sich das Haar damit.
2. Zu Hause ißt man in diesem Zimmer.
3. Auf einem Bett zu sehen. Sehr warm.
4. In diesem Zimmer bereitet man das Essen zu.
5. Es hängt oft an der Wand.
6. In der Küche zu sehen. Käse und Milch findet man darin.
7. Man kann Papier damit schneiden.
8. Man trocknet sich das Haar damit.
9. Im Schlafzimmer zu sehen. Man hängt Kleider darin auf.

35

Exercise 3
Strange Sentences

Can you make corrections to these sentences so that they make better sense?

1. Ich rasiere mich mit einem Schwamm.
2. Ich wache auf, wenn der Kessel klingelt.
3. Meine Schwester schläft normalerweise in der Garage.
4. Unser Haus ist aus Plastik gebaut.
5. Meine Mutter flickt meine Kleider mit einer Zange.
6. Ich koche mir das Abendessen auf einer Heizdecke.
7. Ich öffne Flaschen mit einem Schraubenzieher.
8. Wenn er müde ist, schläft mein Vater in der Tiefkühltruhe.
9. Auf dem Bücherregal habe ich über hundert Plattenspieler.
10. Zum Mittagessen bereitet Mutter eine schöne Kasserolle zu.

Exercise 4
Odd Man Out

Say which word you think is the odd man out in each group below. Give reasons for your answers.

1. Hammer Reißnagel Hobel Bohrgerät
2. Waschmaschine Kühlschrank Kleiderschrank Elektroherd
3. Badewanne Schwamm Seife Toaster
4. Pinsel Gummiband Schnur Tesafilm
5. stopfen flicken fernsehen reparieren
6. Kassettenrecorder Nähmaschine Radio Plattenspieler
7. Kusine Nichte Bruder Erwachsene
8. Zahnpasta Seide Samt Leder
9. Sofa Fernseher Lehnstuhl Schere
10. Backstein Harke Beton Holz

Sport, Hobbies and Relaxation

Leisure and Free Time

der Brieffreund (-e)/ die Brieffreundin (-nen)	pen-friend
die Disco (-s)	disco
der Film (-e)	film
der Fotoapparat (-e)	camera
die Freizeit	free time
das Hobby (-s)	hobby
der Jugendklub (-s)	youth club
das Kino (-s)	cinema
der Krimi (-s)	detective film/story
das Lied (-er)	song
das Modell (-e)	model
die Party (-s)	party
die Photographie	photography
die Postkarte (-n)	postcard
der Roman (-e)	novel
das Wandern	hiking

basteln	to make models
einen Spaziergang machen	to go for a walk
fernsehen	to watch television
lesen	to read
malen	to paint
nähen	to sew
Radio hören	to listen to the radio
sammeln	to collect
singen	to sing
tanzen	to dance
tauschen	to swop, exchange

The World of Music

das Album (Alben)	LP, album
das Cello (-s)	cello
der Dirigent (-en)	conductor
die Flöte (-n)	flute
der Flügel (-)	grand piano
die Geige (-n)	violin
die Gitarre (-n)	guitar
der Jazz	jazz
die Kassette (-n)	cassette
der Kassettenrecorder (-)	cassette tape recorder
die Klarinette (-n)	clarinet
das Klavier (-e)	piano
die (klassische) Musik	(classical) music
der Musiker (die Musikerin)	musician
das Musikinstrument (-e)	musical instrument
die Note (-n)	note
die Oper (-n)	opera
das Opernhaus (=er)	opera house
das Orchester	orchestra ·
die Orgel (-n)	organ
der Plattenspieler (-)	record player
die Popgruppe (-n)	pop group
das Rock-Konzert (-e)	rock concert
die Saite (-n)	string
das Saxophon (-e)	saxophone
die Schallplatte (-n)	record
das Tamburin (-e)	tambourine
die Trommel (-n)	drum
die Trompete (-n)	trumpet
die Volksmusik	folk music

---

ich spiele Klavier	I play the piano
üben	to practise

The Sporting World

das Angeln	fishing
der Basketball	basketball
das Bergsteigen	mountaineering
das Boxen	boxing
der Fan (-s)	fan, supporter
der Federball	badminton
der (Fußball)spieler (-)	(football) player
das Golf	golf
der Handball	handball
das Hangsegeln	hang gliding
das Hockey	hockey
das Jagen	hunting
die Leichtathletik (*sing.*)	athletics
die Mannschaft	team
das Radfahren	cycling
das Reiten	riding
das Rudern	rowing
das Schießen	shooting
der Schläger (-)	racket
das Schlittschuhlaufen	skating
das Schwimmen	swimming
der Ski (-er)	ski
das Spiel (-e)	game
der Sport (-e)	sport
das Stadion (Stadien)	stadium
das Team (-s)	team
der Tennisplatz (-̈e)	tennis court
das (Tisch)tennis	(table) tennis
das Turnen	gymnastics
die Turnhalle (-n)	gymnasium
der Volleyball!	volleyball

Exercise 1
Jumbled Words

Use the clues given to unravel these jumbled German words.

1. Hier hört man laute Musik!   S I D O C
2. Hier kann man abends seine Freunde   D K B J U L G E N U
   treffen.
3. Etwas zum Lesen.   M O R N A
4. Man kann an ihn schreiben. Er wohnt   E F R B I R E U F N D
   vielleicht im Ausland.
5. Man singt es.   D I E L
6. Ein Instrument.   B I M T U A R N
7. Wo große Fußballspiele stattfinden.   T A S D O I N
8. Wenn man nicht arbeitet, hat man . . .   T I Z I F E E R
9. Wenn man in den Ferien ist, schickt   T O P S K A T E R
   man oft eine _____ nach Hause.
10. Im Sommer ist es schön, auf dem   W E D N A R N
    Lande zu . . .

Exercise 2
In your spare time

Some young Germans were asked about their hobbies. These are
the answers they gave . . . or at least part of them. Can you select a
suitable verb from the list below to fill in each blank? Be careful of
the 'decoy' verbs which you won't need!

1. Ich _____ Bücher.
2. Ich _____ fern.
3. Ich _____ Bilder.
4. Ich _____ zur Disco.
5. Ich _____ Lieder.
6. Ich _____ Fotos.
7. Ich _____ an meine Brieffreundin.
8. Ich _____ Kleider.
9. Ich _____ einen Spaziergang auf dem Lande.
10. Ich _____ Klavier.

nähe   jage   mache   schwimme   fahre   singe   spiele   lese
male   sehe   übe   mache   gehe   schreibe

Topic 8
Clothing, the Body and Health

Clothes

der Anorak (-s)	anorak
der Anzug (∺e)	suit
die Badehose (-n)	pair of trunks
der BH	bra
der Bikini (-s)	bikini
die Bluse (-n)	blouse
der Handschuh (-e)	glove
das Hemd (-en)	shirt
die Hose (-n)	pair of trousers
der Hut (∺e)	hat
die Jacke (-n)	jacket
die Jeans *(pl.)*	jeans
das Kleid (-er)	dress
der Mantel (∺)	coat
der Pulli (-s)	pullover, jumper
der Regenmantel (∺)	raincoat
der Rock (∺e)	skirt
die Sandale (-n)	sandal
der Schlafanzug (∺e)	pyjamas
der Schlips (-e)	tie
der Schuh (-e)	shoe
die Socke (-n)	sock
der Stiefel (-)	boot
die Strumpfhose (-n)	pair of tights
das T-shirt	T-shirt
der Trainingsanzug (∺e)	track suit
die Unterhose (-n)	pair of underpants

sich anziehen	to get dressed
sich ausziehen	to get undressed
sich umziehen	to get changed

41

Parts of the Body

der Arm (-e)	arm
das Auge (-n)	eye
die Augenbraue (-n)	eyebrow
das Bein (-e)	leg
der Daumen (-)	thumb
der Ellbogen (-)	elbow
der Finger (-)	finger
der Fuß (Füße)	foot
das Gesicht (-er)	face
das Haar (-e)	hair
der Hals (¨e)	neck
die Hand (¨e)	hand
das Herz (-en)	heart
das Kinn (-e)	chin
das Knie (-n)	knee
der Knochen (-)	bone
der Kopf (¨e)	head
der Körper (-)	body
die Lippe (-n)	lip
der Magen (-)	stomach
der Mund (¨er)	mouth
die Nase (-n)	nose
das Ohr (-en)	ear
der Rücken (-)	back
die Schulter (-n)	shoulder
die Stirn (-en)	forehead
die Wange (-n)	cheek
der Zahn (¨e)	tooth
die Zehe (-n)	toe
die Zunge (-n)	tongue

Health

der Apotheker (-)/	chemist
die Apothekerin (-nen)	
der Arzt (∺e)/die Ärztin (-nen)	doctor
das Aspirin	aspirin
der Atem	breath
die Bauchschmerzen *(pl.)*	tummy ache
das Blut	blood
die Erkältung (-en)	cold
das Fieber (-)	fever
die Gesundheit	health
die Grippe	flu
das Halsweh	sore throat
der Husten	cough
das Kopfweh	headache
das Krankenhaus (∺er)	hospital
der Krankenpfleger (-)/	nurse
die Krankenpflegerin (-nen)	
die Krankenschwester (-n)	nurse
der Krankenwagen (-)	ambulance
die Krankheit (-en)	illness
das Pflaster	plaster
die Pille (-n)	pill
das Rezept (-e)	prescription
das Sprechzimmer (-)	surgery
die Tablette (-n)	tablet
die Temperatur (-en)	temperature
die Tragbahre (-n)	stretcher
die Untersuchung (-en)	examination
die Verletzung (-en)	injury
der Zahnarzt (∺e)	dentist
das Zahnweh	toothache

ich fühle mich krank	I feel ill
in Ohnmacht fallen	to faint

Exercise 1
Coded Clothes

A	B	C	D	E	F	G	H	I	J	K	L	M
1	2	3	4	5	6	7	8	9	10	11	12	13

N	O	P	Q	R	S	T	U	V	W	X	Y	Z
14	15	16	17	18	19	20	21	22	23	24	25	26

Numbers have been used to replace letters in this code, but as an additional complication the words have then been written backwards as well. See how quickly you can decipher these coded clothes.

1. 5 11 3 1 10
2. 9 12 12 21 16
3. 7 21 26 14 1
4. 12 5 6 5 9 20 19
5. 19 14 1 5 10

6. 19 16 9 12 8 3 19
7. 9 14 9 11 9 2
8. 4 9 5 12 11
9. 12 5 20 14 1 13 14 5 7 5 18
10. 5 12 1 4 14 1 19

Exercise 2
Mixed-up Remedies

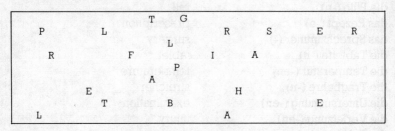

Mixed up together here are *three* German words for things which might very well be useful to you if you were ill or injured – can you unravel them all and write them out correctly with their English meanings?

The World of Food and Drink

Having a Meal

das Abendessen	evening meal
die Dose (-n)	tin
das Essen	meal, food
die Flasche (-n)	bottle
das Frühstück (-e)	breakfast
die Gabel (-n)	fork
das Gericht (-e)	course
das Geschirr	crockery
das Glas (¨er)	glass
die Kaffeekanne (-n)	coffee pot
der Löffel (-)	spoon
die Mahlzeit (-en)	mealtime
das Messer (-)	knife
das Mittagessen (-)	lunch
die Nachspeise (-n)	dessert
der Nachtisch (-e)	dessert
die Schale (-n)	bowl
die Schüssel (-n)	bowl, dish
die Serviette (-n)	serviette
die Tasse (-n)	cup
die Teekanne (-n)	teapot
der Teller (-)	plate
das Tischtuch (¨er)	tablecloth
die Untertasse (-n)	saucer
die Vorspeise (-n)	starter course

Guten Appetit!/Prost!	enjoy your meal!/cheers!
ich decke den Tisch/ich räume den Tisch ab	I lay the table/clear the table
ich esse/trinke gern	I like eating/drinking . . .
ich habe Durst/Hunger	I'm thirsty/hungry
ich mag	I'like

Food and Drink (1)

der Apfelsaft	apple juice
das Bier	beer
das Bonbon (-s)	sweet
das Brötchen (-)	bread roll
die Butter	butter
das Butterbrot	piece of bread and butter
der Champagner	champagne
die Chips *(pl.)*	crisps
die Cola	cola
das Ei (-er)	egg
der Eintopf	thick soup (served as main course)
das Eis	ice
der Essig	vinegar
der Fisch (-e)	fish
das Fleisch	meat
die Frikadelle (-n)	meat rissole
der Fruchtsaft (:e)	fruit juice
das Getränk (-e)	drink
das Hähnchen (-)	chicken
der Honig	honey
der Joghurt (-s)	yoghurt
der Kaffee	coffee
der Kakao	cocoa
das Kalbfleisch	veal
der Käse (-)	cheese
der Keks (-e)	biscuit
der Kognak (-s)	brandy
das Kotelett (-e)	chop
der Kuchen (-)	cake
die Leber	liver
die Limonade	lemonade

Food and Drink (2)

die Margarine	margarine
die Marmelade (-n)	marmelade
die Milch	milk
das Omelett (-s)	omelette
der Paprika	paprika, red pepper
der Pfeffer	pepper
die Pommes Frites *(pl.)*	chips
der Reis	rice
das Rindfleisch	beef
die Sahne	cream
der Salat (-e)	salad
das Salz	salt
die Sauce (-n)	sauce
der Schinken	ham
die Schokolade (-n)	chocolate
die Schlagsahne	whipped cream
das Schnitzel (-)	cutlet
das Schwarzbrot	rye bread
das Schweinefleisch	pork
der Senf	mustard
der Speck	bacon
das Spiegelei (-er)	fried egg
das Steak (-s)	steak
die Suppe (-n)	soup
der Tee	tea
der Toast (-s)	toast
das Wasser	water
der Wein (-e)	wine
der Whisky (-s)	whisky
die Wurst (-e)	sausage
der Zucker	sugar

Fruit and Nuts

die Ananas (-se)	pineapple
der Apfel (⸚)	apple
die Apfelsine (-n)	orange
die Aprikose (-n)	apricot
die Banane (-n)	banana
die Beere (-n)	berry
die Birne (-n)	pear
die Erdbeere (-n)	strawberry
die Erdnuß (Erdnüsse)	peanut
die Haselnuß (Haselnüsse)	hazelnut
die Himbeere (-n)	raspberry
die Kirsche (-n)	cherry
die Melone (-n)	melon
die Nuß (Nüsse)	nut
das Obst	fruit
die Pampelmuse (-n)	grapefruit
der Pfirsich (-e)	peach
die Pflaume (-n)	plum
die Stachelbeere (-n)	gooseberry
die Trauben (pl.)	grapes
die Walnuß (Walnüsse)	walnut
die Zitrone (-n)	lemon

bitter	bitter
hart	hard
reif	ripe
saftig	juicy
süß	sweet
trocken	dry
unreif	unripe
weich	soft

Vegetables

der Blumenkohl (-e)	cauliflower
die Bohne (-n)	bean
der Braunkohl	broccoli
die Brunnenkresse	watercress
die Erbse (-n)	pea
die Gurke (-n)	cucumber
die Karotte (-n)	carrot
die Kartoffel (-n)	potato
der Kohl (-e)	cabbage
der Kopfsalat (-e)	lettuce
der Kürbis (-se)	pumpkin
der Lauch (-e)	leek
die Paprikaschote (-n)	red or green peppers
die Petersilie	parsley
der Pilz (-e)	mushroom
das Radieschen (-)	red radish
der Rosenkohl *(sing.)*	Brussels sprouts
die Rübe (-n)	swede
das Sauerkraut	pickled cabbage
der Spargel	asparagus
der Spinat	spinach
die Stangenbohne (-n)	runner bean
die Tomate (-n)	tomato
die weiße Rübe (-n)	turnip
die Zwiebel (-n)	onion

Exercise 1
Food and drink word search

This puzzle is concealing at least *thirty* items of food and drink in German. The words are written horizontally, vertically, diagonally, backwards or forwards.

How many can you find?

K	J	Z	J	G	M	Y	V	L	F	T	F	A	S	N	E	G	N	A	R	O	V	C	G	E
H	W	K	N	L	U	M	T	U	V	O	O	E	N	M	O	L	B	A	P	U	Z	W	B	Y
I	F	L	E	I	S	C	H	W	T	X	K	N	W	Z	L	D	Z	C	T	X	Y	A	X	Z
Z	Y	O	T	X	X	R	U	Q	T	P	S	L	S	M	S	C	H	I	N	K	E	N	Y	U
A	D	Z	R	A	X	Y	O	Q	P	Z	S	J	R	R	V	K	K	D	Y	S	W	R	V	X
S	B	C	H	Z	L	A	S	U	M	N	W	Q	S	L	P	D	R	J	C	H	G	B	A	B
P	Z	A	Q	P	B	H	R	F	X	Q	R	U	Y	M	Q	O	J	U	C	I	Z	E	T	A
I	C	S	Z	W	I	E	B	E	L	I	G	I	R	F	X	M	N	E	N	H	E	B	Q	C
E	W	P	B	L	S	O	C	V	P	S	T	Y	H	S	G	T	N	Q	I	F	G	A	D	W
G	Y	B	D	U	P	N	A	U	W	V	H	N	M	D	T	L	E	M	F	O	D	P	F	S
E	R	I	V	T	X	I	L	A	T	R	I	L	I	H	U	F	P	A	N	E	F	V	O	B
L	F	E	E	W	G	V	O	M	L	E	D	J	E	H	M	E	K	V	P	W	O	E	F	N
E	Q	R	E	V	F	K	C	J	O	F	U	Z	K	F	Z	G	A	G	B	T	G	X	H	E
I	H	A	Z	F	Q	H	S	W	I	F	B	I	M	C	G	S	Z	A	P	C	O	K	I	X
Q	X	Q	P	W	Y	S	G	X	V	E	J	T	K	T	S	U	P	P	E	U	Q	I	S	L
F	G	T	A	L	A	S	I	Z	J	F	Y	R	X	V	Y	D	L	R	H	B	D	W	C	J
G	H	E	B	D	R	J	L	J	F	P	K	O	N	O	U	J	N	K	O	C	J	V	H	D
F	D	R	O	C	U	T	C	W	X	K	P	N	F	K	L	E	F	R	L	L	M	X	L	K
E	I	H	R	E	T	T	U	B	G	Q	V	E	P	E	J	U	M	K	I	E	U	C	A	V
G	I	V	S	N	G	K	H	M	I	J	A	R	K	D	B	P	T	C	F	K	P	M	G	H
E	J	X	L	S	M	C	W	I	J	E	Q	C	J	A	I	G	E	A	D	A	Y	W	S	T
I	W	Z	O	D	Z	M	E	Y	U	L	F	K	D	N	T	H	E	T	J	R	N	G	A	F
S	K	S	T	U	T	L	N	M	F	L	B	R	Q	O	B	I	A	B	E	O	C	B	H	Z
H	E	P	Y	V	H	Y	H	D	I	K	I	E	V	M	S	E	S	F	D	T	A	B	N	S
Y	A	R	O	B	S	N	O	M	S	Q	R	N	A	I	X	G	Y	U	Q	T	D	C	E	A
A	I	P	A	Z	C	T	B	V	C	N	N	G	H	L	L	F	V	B	D	E	O	Z	A	P
O	J	Q	F	Q	N	A	Z	U	H	B	E	L	G	W	F	W	H	E	X	A	H	Y	E	A
B	N	F	G	E	W	X	L	I	O	K	K	B	X	M	O	R	C	P	W	S	G	Q	E	F
Z	D	Y	M	U	L	J	R	P	B	A	N	A	N	E	S	T	O	R	B	C	I	T	S	R
C	E	I	R	X	K	W	M	J	W	E	U	N	Y	O	Z	N	L	O	I	P	B	E	B	R
P	C	R	D	K	A	R	T	O	F	F	E	L	G	H	M	J	Q	X	N	U	Y	V	R	C
A	Q	B	X	S	W	V	U	Q	T	V	R	S	R	K	I	R	S	M	T	D	O	A	D	P
Z	T	Y	S	A	N	A	N	A	F	S	Y	P	T	H	S	E	N	F	Z	N	U	O	Q	Z

Exercise 2
Odd Man Out

Decide which word you think is the odd man out in each of the
following groups of words. Give reasons for your answers.

1. Tee   Kaffee   Pfeffer   Wasser
2. Whisky   Cola   Wein   Bier
3. Kalbfleisch   Senf   Leber   Schinken
4. Pfirsich   Blumenkohl   Pilz   Karotte
5. Eis   Suppe   Joghurt   Kuchen
6. reif   trocken   grau   süß
7. Toast   Salz   Essig   Pfeffer
8. Margarine   Butter   Bonbon   Honig
9. Trauben   Zitrone   Apfel   Walnuß
10. Schnitzel   Reis   Speck   Rindfleisch

Exercise 3
Making food and drink

| S | T | A | C | H | E | L | B | E | E | R | E |
| S | C | H | W | E | I | N | E | F | L | E | I | S | C | H |

You may use the letters in the above two words as many times as
you want – but *only* these letters. Mix the words together as you
wish. See how many kinds of food and drink you can make up in
German using these letters.

Topic 10
Miscellaneous

Cities of Europe

Amsterdam	Amsterdam
Athen	Athens
Basel	Basle
Berlin	Berlin
Bern	Berne
Bonn	Bonn
Brüssel	Brussels
Genf	Geneva
Frankfurt-am-Main	Frankfurt-am-Main
Hamburg	Hamburg
Köln	Cologne
Kopenhagen	Copenhagen
Lissabon	Lisbon
London	London
Madrid	Madrid
Mailand	Milan
Moskau	Moscow
München	Munich
Neapel	Naples
Nürnberg	Nuremberg
Oslo	Oslo
Paris	Paris
Prag	Prague
Rom	Rome
Stockholm	Stockholm
Stuttgart	Stuttgart
Venedig	Venice
Warschau	Warsaw
Wien	Vienna
Zürich	Zurich

Countries and Continents

Afrika	Africa
Amerika	America
Asien	Asia
Australien	Australia
Belgien	Belgium
BRD (die Bundesrepublik Deutschland)	West Germany
Dänemark	Denmark
DDR (die Deutsche Demokratische Republik)	East Germany
England	England
Europa	Europe
Frankreich	France
Großbritannien	Great Britain
Holland	Holland
Irland	Ireland
Italien	Italy
Kanada	Canada
Japan	Japan
Luxemburg	Luxemburg
Norwegen	Norway
Österreich	Austria
Polen	Poland
Portugal	Portugal
Schottland	Scotland
Schweden	Sweden
die Sowjetunion (die UdSSR)	USSR
Spanien	Spain
die Schweiz	Switzerland
die Tschechoslowakei	Czechoslovakia
die Vereinigten Staaten (die USA)	USA
Wales	Wales

Time

der Abend (-e)	evening
der Augenblick (-e)	moment
das Datum (Daten)	date
das Jahr (-e)	year
das Jahrhundert (-e)	century
die Minute (-n)	minute
der Moment (-e)	moment
der Monat (-e)	month
der Morgen (-)	morning
der Nachmittag (-e)	afternoon
die Nacht (¨e)	night
die Stunde (-n)	hour
der Tag (-e)	day
die Woche (-n)	week
das Wochenende (-n)	weekend
die Zeit (-en)	time

---

am nächsten Tag	on the next day
der Wievielte ist heute?	what is the date today?
es ist punkt 3	it is exactly 3 o'clock
es ist viertel vor/nach 8	it is quarter to/past 8
früh/spät/pünktlich	early/late/punctual(ly)
gegen/um 7 Uhr	about/at 7 o'clock
gestern/vorgestern	yesterday/the day before yesterday
um halb fünf	at half past four
heute/heute abend	today/this evening
meine Uhr geht vor/nach	my watch is fast/slow
morgen	tomorrow
morgens/abends/nachmittags	in the mornings/eveings/afternoons
täglich	daily
wieviel Uhr ist es?	what time is it?

Quantities

die Büchse (-n)	can; tin
das Dutzend (-e)	dozen
das Faß (Fässer)	barrel
die Flasche (-n)	bottle
das Glas (⁼er)	glass
die Kanne (-n)	pot
das Kilo (-s)	kilo
das Liter (-)	litre
das Meter (-)	metre
das Paar (-e)	pair
die Packung (-en)	packet
das Pfund (-e)	pound
die Portion (-en)	portion
der Riegel (-)	bar (of chocolate, soap)
die Schachtel (-n)	packet
die Scheibe (-n)	slice
das Stück (-e)	piece
die Tafel (-n)	bar or block (of chocolate)
die Tasse (-n)	cup
der Würfel (-)	cube

ein bißchen	a little
ein halbes Kilo	half a kilo
ein halbes Liter	half a litre
ein halbes Pfund	half a pound
etwas	some
hundert Gramm	one hundred grams

Days, Months, Seasons, Holidays

der Frühling	Spring
der Sommer	Summer
der Herbst	Autumn
der Winter	Winter

Januar	January
Februar	February
März	March
April	April
Mai	May
Juni	June
Juli	July
August	August
September	September
Oktober	October
November	November
Dezember	December

Montag	Monday
Dienstag	Tuesday
Mittwoch	Wednesday
Donnerstag	Thursday
Freitag	Friday
Samstag (*Sonnabend*)	Saturday
Sonntag	Sunday

Palmsonntag	Palm Sunday
Ostersonntag/montag	Easter Sunday/Monday
Karfreitag	Good Friday
Neujahrstag	New Year's Day
zu Pfingsten/Ostern/ Weihnachten	at Whitsun/Easter/Christmas
Silvesterabend	New Year's Eve
Weihnachtsabend/tag	Christmas Eve/Day

Cardinal Numbers

null	0
eins	1
zwei	2
drei	3
vier	4
fünf	5
sechs	6
sieben	7
acht	8
neun	9
zehn	10
elf	11
zwölf	12
dreizehn	13
vierzehn	14
fünfzehn	15
sechzehn	16
siebzehn	17
achtzehn	18
neunzehn	19
zwanzig	20
einundzwanzig	21
zweiundzwanzig *etc.*	22
dreißig	30
vierzig	40
fünfzig	50
sechzig	60
siebzig	70
achtzig	80
neunzig	90
hundert	100
hunderteins *etc.*	101
zweihundert	200
tausend	1,000
tausendeins *etc.*	1,001
zweitausend	2,000
hunderttausend	100,000
eine Million	1,000,000
drei Millionen	3,000,000

Ordinal Numbers

der Erste	1st
der Zweite	2nd
der Dritte	3rd
der Vierte	4th
der Fünfte	5th
der Sechste	6th
der Siebente	7th
der Achte	8th
der Neunte	9th
der Zehnte	10th
der Elfte	11th
der Zwölfte	12th
der Dreizehnte	13th
der Vierzehnte	14th
der Fünfzehnte	15th
der Sechzehnte	16th
der Siebzehnte	17th
der Achtzehnte	18th
der Neunzehnte	19th
der Zwanzigste	20th
der Einundzwanzigste	21st
der Zweiundzwanzigste *etc.*	22nd
der Dreißigste	30th
der Vierzigste	40th
der Fünfzigste	50th
der Sechzigste	60th
der Siebzigste	70th
der Achtzigste	80th
der Neunzigste	90th
der Hundertste	100th
der Hunderterste	101st
der Hundertzehnte	110th
der Zweihundertste	200th
der Tausendste	1,000th
der Zweitausendste	2,000th
der Millionste	1,000,000th
der Dreimillionste	3,000,000th

58

Colours

beige	beige
blau	blue
braun	brown
bräunlich	tan
creme	cream
gelb	yellow
golden	golden
grau	grey
grün	green
himmelblau	sky blue
karminrot	crimson
königsblau	royal blue
lila	mauve
marineblau	navy blue
orangenfarben	orange
purpurrot	purple
rosa	pink
rot	red
scharlachrot	scarlet
schwarz	black
silbern	silver
smaragdgrün	emerald green
türkisfarben	turquoise
veilchenblau	violet
violett	purple
weiß	white

dunkelgrün	dark green
hellgrün	light green

Describing People

alt	old
arm	poor
dick	fat
dumm	stupid
dünn	thin
elegant	elegant
faul	lazy
fleißig	hard-working
freundlich	friendly
geduldig	patient
glücklich	happy
groß	tall, big
häßlich	ugly
höflich	polite
hübsch	pretty
intelligent	intelligent
jung	young
klein	small
klug	clever
müde	tired
nett	nice, kind
reich	rich
schön	beautiful
schlank	slim
schwach	weak
stark	strong
stolz	proud
sympathisch	nice, pleasant
traurig	sad
ungezogen	naughty

Describing Things (1)

alt	old
außerordentlich	extraordinary
beliebt	popular, well-liked
berühmt	famous
breit	wide
bunt	brightly-coloured
dunkel	dark
eng	narrow
falsch	wrong
frei	free, vacant
frisch	fresh
gefährlich	dangerous
gut	good
heiß	hot
herrlich	magnificent
hoch	high
interessant	interesting
kalt	cold
klar	clear
komisch	funny, amusing
kühl	cool
kurz	short
lang	long
langsam	slow
langweilig	boring
laut	loud, noisy
leer	empty
modern	modern
neu	new
ordentlich	tidy

Describing Things (2)

reif	ripe
rein	clean
richtig	right, correct
ruhig	calm
rund	round
sanft	soft, gentle
sauber	clean
scharf	sharp
schlecht	bad
schlimm	bad
schmal	narrow
schmutzig	dirty
schnell	quick
schrecklich	frightful
schwer	heavy
schwierig	difficult
seltsam	strange
spannend	exciting
still	quiet
süß	sweet
tief	deep
trocken	dry
unmöglich	impossible
viereckig	square
wahr	true
warm	warm
weich	soft
weit	far
wichtig	important
wild	wild
wunderbar	wonderful

Common Verbs (1)

anfangen	to begin
ankommen	to arrive
antworten	to answer
anziehen	to attract
aufwachen	to wake up
ausgeben	to spend
ausrufen	to shout out
sich ausruhen	to rest
sich beeilen	to hurry
befehlen *(+ Dat.)*	to order
begegnen *(+ Dat.)*	to meet
bekommen	to get
bemerken	to notice
beobachten	to observe
beschreiben	to describe
besitzen	to possess
bestehen aus *(+ Dat.)*	to consist of
bestellen	to order
besuchen	to visit
biegen	to bend, turn
bieten	to offer
binden	to tie
bitten (um)	to ask (for)
bleiben	to stay
blicken auf *(+ Acc.)*	to look at
brauchen	to need
brechen	to break
brennen	to burn
bringen	to bring

Common Verbs (2)

danken *(+ Dat.)*	to thank
dauern	to last
denken an *(+ Acc.)*	to think about
dürfen	to be allowed
eilen	to hurry
einladen	to invite
eintreten in *(+ Acc.)*	to enter
empfehlen	to recommend
entdecken	to discover
sich entscheiden	to decide
sich erinnern an *(+ Acc.)*	to remember
erkennen	to recognise
erreichen	to reach
erschrecken	to frighten
erstaunen	to astonish
erwarten	to expect
erzählen	to tell
fallen	to fall
fangen	to catch
finden	to find
flüstern	to whisper
fragen	to ask
sich freuen auf *(+Acc.)*	to look forward to
sich freuen über *(+ Acc.)*	to be pleased about
führen	to lead
sich fürchten vor *(+ Dat.)*	to be afraid of
geben	to give
gefallen *(+ Dat.)*	to please
gehen	to go
gehören *(+ Dat.)*	to belong
gelingen *(+ Dat.)*	to succeed

Common Verbs (3)

gern haben	to like
geschehen	to happen
glauben	to believe
halten	to hold, stop
hangen	to be hanging
hassen	to hate
helfen *(+ Dat.)*	to help
sich hinsetzen	to sit down
hoffen	to hope
holen	to fetch
hören	to hear
sich interessieren **für**	to be interested in
kennen	to know
klettern	to climb
klingeln	to ring
können	to be able
kriegen	to get
lassen	to let, to leave
laufen	to run
leben	to live
legen	to lay
lesen	to read
lieben	to love
liegen	to be lying
malen	to paint
meinen	to think, to believe
mieten	to hire
mögen	to like
müssen	to have to
sich nähern *(+ Dat.)*	to approach

Common Verbs (4)

nehmen	to take
nennen	to name
öffnen	to open
plaudern	to chat
reisen	to travel
rennen	to run
retten	to rescue
riechen nach	to smell of
rufen	to call
sagen	to say
scheinen	to seem, to shine
schlafen	to sleep
schlagen	to hit
schließen	to shut
schneiden	to cut
schreiben	to write
schreien	to yell
schweigen	to be silent
sehen	to see
sein	to be
sich setzen	to sit down
singen	to sing
sitzen	to be sitting
sollen	to ought
spazierengehen	to go for a walk
stehen	to stand
steigen	to climb
stellen	to place, to ask
sterben	to die
stoßen	to push

Common Verbs (5)

suchen nach	to search for
tanzen	to dance
tragen	to carry, to wear
treffen	to meet
tun	to do
überraschen	to surprise
unterbrechen	to interrupt
verbringen	to spend (time)
vergessen	to forget
verlieren	to lose
verschwinden	to disappear
versprechen	to promise
verstehen	to understand
versuchen	to try
sich vorstellen	to introduce oneself
wachsen	to grow
wählen	to choose, to dial
warten auf *(+ Acc.)*	to wait for
sich waschen	to wash oneself
wechseln	to change
werden	to become
werfen	to throw
wissen	to know
wohnen	to live
wollen	to want
zeigen	to show, to point
ziehen	to pull
zuhören *(+ Dat.)*	to listen to
zurückkehren	to turn back
zurückkommen	to come back

Useful Adverbs (1)

am besten	best of all
am liebsten	most of all
auf einmal	suddenly
außerdem	besides
bald	soon
besser	better
dahin	to there
danach	afterwards
dann	then
deshalb	for that reason
dort	there
draußen	outside
eigentlich	really
endlich	finally
erstens	first of all
fast	almost
freilich	of course
früh	early
ganz	completely
genau	exactly
genug	enough
geradeaus	straight on
gern	happily
gewöhnlich	usually
glücklicherweise	fortunately
gut	well

Useful Adverbs (2)

heutzutage	these days
hier	here
hinten	behind, at the back
hoffentlich	hopefully
immer	always
inzwischen	in the meantime
jedenfalls	in any case
jetzt	now
kaum	hardly
keineswegs	no way, by no means
langsam	slowly
leider	unfortunately
lieber	preferably
links	on the left, to the left
manchmal	sometimes
mehr	more
meistens	mostly
mitten (in) *(+ Dat.)*	in the middle (of)
nachher	afterwards
nie	never
noch	yet, still
noch einmal	once more
normalerweise	normally
nun	now
nur	only
oben	upstairs, above
oft	often

Useful Adverbs (3)

plötzlich	suddenly
rechts	on the right, to the right
schlecht	badly
schnell	quickly
schrecklich	terribly
sehr	very
selbst	even
sofort	immediately
sogar	even
sogleich	at once
sonst	otherwise
spät	late
überall	everywhere
ungefähr	about
unten	below, downstairs
unterwegs	on the way
viel	much
vielleicht	perhaps
vorher	before, previously
wahrscheinlich	probably
wann	when
warum	why
wie	how
wo	where
ziemlich	rather
zu	too
zuerst	first of all
zum Beispiel (zB)	for example
zweitens	secondly

Useful Prepositions and Conjunctions (1)

aber	but
als	when
als ob	as if
also	therefore
anstatt *(+ Gen.)*	instead of
auf	on
aus *(+ Dat.)*	out of
außer *(+ Dat.)*	except
bei *(+ Dat.)*	at the home of
durch *(+Acc.)*	through
bevor	before
bis	until
da	since, as
damit	in order that
denn	because
entweder . . . oder	either . . . or
für *(+ Acc.)*	for
gegenüber *(+ Dat.)*	opposite
hinter	behind
in	in
indem	while, as
mit	with
nach	after, to
nachdem	after

Useful Prepositions and Conjunctions (2)

neben	near, next to
nicht nur . . . sondern auch	not only . . . but also
ob	if, whether
obwohl/obgleich	although
oder	or
ohne *(+ Acc.)*	without
seit	since
sobald	as soon as
sondern	but (on the contrary)
trotz (+ Gen.)	in spite of
um	around
und	and
unter	under, among
während	whilst
während *(+ Gen.)*	during
weder . . . noch	neither . . . nor
wegen *(+ Gen.)*	because of
weil/denn	because
wenn	when, if
von	of from
vor	in front of, before
zu	to

Exercise 1
Capitals of the World

Was ist die Hauptstadt ...

1. von Frankreich?
2. von Italien?
3. von Großbritannien?
4. von Belgien?
5. von der Bundesrepublik?
6. von Spanien?
7. von Österreich?
8. von der Schweiz?
9. von Dänemark?
10. von Polen?

Exercise 2
Quantities

Can you match up the items below with the quantities in which you
might want them? For example, you might ask for *eine Tasse Tee*.
Now try the others.

eine Tasse	Tee
ein Glas	Zucker
eine Kanne	Pommes Frites
ein Kilo	Schokolade
eine Portion	Butter
eine Schachtel	Salz
eine Tafel	Wein
500 Gramm	Brot
ein bißchen	Kaffee
eine Scheibe	Zigaretten

Exercise 3
Number Practice

Read out these numbers in German as quickly as you can. If you
stumble or get one wrong, start all over again!

10	15	17	21	33	40
49	58	64	76	80	99
102	210	500	1,000	1,050	5,150
200,000	3,500,000				

Exercise 4
It's just the opposite!

What is the opposite of *jung*? Answer: *alt*!
See how many more pairs of opposites you know by completing this
exercise.

1. Arm ist er nicht! Er hat viel Geld. Er ist sehr _____.
2. Viele Leute halten sie für schön. Ich aber finde sie _____.
3. Dumm! Nicht im geringsten! Sie ist höchst _____.
4. Gestern war er glücklich. Heute aber sieht er ziemlich _____
   aus.
5. Anna ist sehr klein, aber Bärbel ist ganz _____.
6. Peter ist ein höfliches Kind. Sein Bruder aber ist immer _____.
7. Mein Vater ist sehr dick, meine Mutter aber ist sehr _____.
8. Er ist fleißig. Seine Frau steht aber erst um 10 Uhr auf. Sie ist sehr
   _____.

Exercise 5
Describing People

Choose a suitable adjective to complete the following sentences.
1. Seine Tante trägt immer sehr schöne Kleider. Sie ist sehr _____.
2. Sie ißt fast nichts. Deswegen sieht sie so _____ aus.
3. Er geht sehr früh ins Bett. Warum ist er denn immer so _____?
4. Jedes Jahr macht er mir ein schönes Geburtstagsgeschenk. Er ist
   wirklich sehr _____.
5. Er trug die beiden Koffer, obgleich sie sehr schwer sind. Er muß
   sehr _____ sein!

Exercise 6
Choosing the right word

Complete the following sentences with suitable adjectives.

1. Viele Leute mögen seine Filme. Dieser Schauspieler ist in Deutschland sehr _____.
2. Im Winter ist es um 5 Uhr abends schon _____.
3. Entschuldigen Sie, aber diese Antwort ist ganz _____.
4. Es tut mir leid, dieser Platz ist leider nicht _____.
5. Ja, ich sitze gern hier auf dem Balkon. Die Aussicht über die Stadt ist _____.
6. Haben Sie diesen Artikel in der Zeitung gelesen? Er ist sehr _____.
7. Ich fliege immer nach Berlin. Die Zugfahrt dauert zu _____.
8. Im Wohnzimmer war es mir ein bißchen zu heiß, aber hier im Garten ist es schön _____.
9. Mein Lieblingsfach ist Deutsch. Physik aber halte ich für sehr _____.
10. Sie muß fleißig arbeiten. Ihr Haus sieht immer so _____ aus.

Exercise 7
Matching Adjectives

Can you match the items in the left-hand column with a suitable adjective selected from the right-hand column?

Der Apfel ist	schlecht
Der Sand ist	schmutzig
Das Messer ist	so weich
Meine Note in Französisch ist	zu süß
Der Hund ist	schrecklich
Seine Kleider sind	spannend
Der Wein ist	reif
Die erste Vorstellung war	ganz wild
Ich fand diese Geschichte	sehr tief
Das Wasser im Schwimmbad ist	so scharf

Exercise 8
Doing the opposite!

Give a verb which would be opposite in meaning to:

1. gehen
2. kaufen
3. bringen
4. antworten
5. bekommen
6. brechen
7. fallen
8. finden
9. lieben
10. sich setzen

Exercise 9
Verb Practice

Complete the following sentences with a verb which will make good sense.

1. Also, Sie haben diesen Mann gesehen? Können Sie ihn bitte _____?
2. Sie machen jeden Abend so viel Lärm! Ich kann nicht _____.
3. Bis später! Ich muß jetzt einen Brief an meine Freundin _____.
4. Die See ist ganz ruhig. Möchtest du ein Ruderboot _____?
5. Es ist jetzt Punkt zwei. Wann _____ wir London?
6. Entschuldigen Sie bitte, diese zwei Koffer _____ mir.
7. Die Tür ist geschlossen, und ich kann sie mit diesem Schlüssel nicht _____.
8. Können Sie mir bitte dieses englische Geld in D-Mark _____?
9. Er spricht so schnell, ich kann ihn nicht _____.
10. Guten Morgen. Ich heiße Blank. Darf ich Ihnen meinen Freund _____?

Exercise 10
Adverb Opposites

See if you can match the adverbs in the left-hand column with their opposites chosen from the right-hand column.

dort	glücklicherweise
endlich	spät
schnell	nie
links	schlecht
vorher	erstens
leider	oben
immer	hier
unten	nachher
früh	rechts
gut	langsam

LONGMAN GROUP UK LIMITED
Longman House
Burnt Mill, Harlow, Essex CM20 2JE, England
and Associated Companies throughout the World

First published 1986

Set in 10/12pt Rockwell Light (Linotron)

Produced by Longman Group (F.E.) Limited
Printed in Hong Kong

ISBN 0-582-20349-X